DOGS HEALTH

The Perfect Handbook
for Imperfect Dog Owners

Jack M. Davis

TABLE OF CONTENTS

PRELUDE

Dogs are an integral part of human society on every inhabited continent on Earth. They drive livestock and protect it; police property; scent and detect illicit substances; haul sleds; retrieve game; guide the blind; search for and rescue the lost and injured; comfort the lonely; hear for the deaf, or add a sparkling natural reality to the lives of hundreds of millions of people throughout the world.

As we move from an agrarian to urban culture, dogs are in many ways one of our last and most important links with the natural world. We get pleasure from caring for our gardens and our pets.

This e-book on "Perfect handbook for imperfect dog owners" emphasizes the pet

4

owner to offer good care to his or her pet and also gives solutions for unresolved problems.

CHAPTER 1

UNDERSTANDING INGREDIENTS

Understanding the ingredients of your dog's food items is a must for dog lovers or dog owners. Whenever you feed the dog with different kinds of food items, you should always read the label and understand the contents of the dog feed types used in such commercial preparations. You should understand the ingredients while buying food for your dog and also know what to look for.

Feed items include dry and fresh food. The new dog food prepared in homes generally consists of ingredients like freshly cut chicken pieces and cranberry juices, blue-green algae, etc.

If you come across any different preservatives and if the dog develops sudden signs about the food allergy, suspect the unwanted ingredient in the feed items. Similarly, understand the moisture status. If the food item has more moisture, then the dog may prefer this as well.

Beet pulp, pasta, Soybean oil, wheat middlings, calcium carbonate, magnesium oxide, copper sulfate, iron sulfate, zinc oxide, choline chloride, etc. case of vegetarian-based diet items, offered to pet animals like dogs.

Raw egg, chicken, beef, mutton, fish, quail, etc., are often the preferred ingredients in dog diets prepared based on non-vegetarian items. Taurine is one of the essential ingredients for the dog's nutrition. Likewise, in dogs feed with frozen fish items, the vitamin called thiamine needs to be supplemented as an ingredient.

Many dog food preparations contain essential fatty acids, carbohydrates with adequate fiber contents, vitamins like A, D, E, and B complex vitamins.

Furthermore, minerals like zinc are an essential ingredient for skin health status, and calcium, a necessary component for bone growth and tonicity of muscles. They should be enriched in these food items. However, those food preparations are comparatively more expensive than the food preparations with general ingredients. However, it may be better for your dog's health.

CHAPTER 2

DOGS NEED DIFFERENT DIETS AT DIFFERENT AGES

Dogs need different diets at different ages. Yes. This is true. For example, the puppy needs milk as the primary food item, while an adult dog may need beef or chicken in addition to the boiled egg and milk. Depending on the age factor, the diet schedule varies in reality for the dogs like any other species.

Puppies need more significant amounts of protein, fat, and carbohydrates than an adult dog. Furthermore, puppies need more frequent feeding schedules in a day, unlike an adult dog. The movement-based diet requirements are more in puppies since they are often more active than adult dogs.

Elder dogs need restricted protein, but the protein needs to be easily digestible and easily assimilated into the body. The diet schedule should have an ample supply of water for them. Feeding aged dogs too much protein may finally lead to an overburden of the renal structures, and ultimately, the dog may end up damaging filters in the kidney.

This is true significantly when the immune system of these dogs is compromised due to many factors. Similarly, the elderly dogs need less food only because the movements of the adult dogs are highly restricted, and hence, they have to spend a limited of energy.

Female dogs in the pregnancy stage need not be fed a full stomach since it may cause some discomfort to the animal. However, the pregnant animal and the nursing animal need a particular food item that delivers a balanced nutrition supplement with proper supplementation of vitamins and minerals.

The nursing animal with puppies needs to be fed with enough amounts of calcium, and hence, there will not be any calcium-based deficiency, and the bones of the puppies will be strong without any curving.

CHAPTER 3

VITAMIN AND MINERAL SUPPLEMENTS

Vitamin and mineral supplements are essential components in any dog's feeding. If there is a balance in the vitamin and mineral supplements, then the animal will have a healthy life, and hence, the immunity is not compromised in an unwanted way. This means that there the dog will be more disease resistant to various diseases.

Pet owners should know that vitamins A, D, E, and K are fat-soluble vitamins and others are water-soluble vitamins. Vitamins like thiamine, pyridoxine, and cyanocobalamin are essential for the functions of the nervous system. Vitamin A deficiency leads to night blindness, skin lesions, and vitamin D deficiency, leading to the softening and weakening of the bones.

These problems are many a time encountered by dog owners. Among these, vitamin A toxicities may occur if you feed them in excessive amounts, like vitamin D. Hence, emphasize this while using these vitamins in the dogs. Cod liver oil from selected fishes has more vitamin A in them and is a universally good feed for dogs.

All dogs may not need vitamins or vitamins to live well for the moment, but it is essential for their future. If they become sick or aged, or very young without proper feeding, supplementations are required to upkeep their health status. However, one has to follow the instructions of a veterinarian in this regard.

If the dogs are fed with fish in freezing conditions, they may constantly be suffering from vitamin B1 deficiency, and hence, such dogs need to be explicitly given B1. Careless supplementations of minerals may lead to diseases, and hence, veterinarians always need to be consulted on the supplementation of minerals or vitamins.

Minerals like calcium, magnesium, zinc, manganese, iron, copper, etc., are given more emphasis and sodium and potassium. Zinc is related to skin health and potassium is associated with muscle health, and calcium with phosphorus is associated with bone health.

However, if you feed the dog with chicken, mutton, or beef along with required vegetables, artificial supplementation of mineral or vitamin tablets may be highly reduced. Still, supplements need to be considered when you cannot maintain balanced nutrition, as this happens with most dogs due to multifaceted causes.

CHAPTER 4

BOREDOM AND VARIETY

Boredom and variety are always inter-connected in case of dog misbehaving. Yes. This is true. Often, boredom can be managed with various materials that will distract the animals to a greater extent. Hence, the dog may not do the abnormal or unwanted activity arising out of its boredom.

Boredom-experienced dogs may have different types of behavioral patterns. For example, some dogs will be seen barking continuously, and some may always be engaged in some digging activities.

There are many ways to get your dog out of its boredom activities. Many toys are available, which simulated duck, dog, rodent, etc.

These may be kept inside the crate, and in particular, puppies love these items. A buster cube with multiple treats may be placed in the dog's shelter, and the animal soon understands how to roll the buster cube to get the treats it prefers. A Buster Cube is an ingenious toy use for simulating and activating your dog during play and feed time. Instead of placing the food monotonously in one place, change the place of providing suddenly.

Such actions will help remove the boredom-like activity in your dog. Activities about boredom need to be redefined well by the dog owners. This will help them to a greater extent to drive away from the unwanted behavior patterns in their pet dogs.

For example, some dogs may often have destructive biting characters and will be seen biting chairs, cloth, mats, and everything they can see. After ruling out the teething problem, if it is a puppy, provide it with some large-sized balls, mineral mixture-based bone materials, etc. Such a variety of materials help to reduce boredom-related activities.

CHAPTER 5

COST OF FEEDS

The cost of dog feed is one factor that is most important in the case of feeding dogs with different kinds of food items. Yes. This is true. The cost factor needs to be looked into in various perspectives during the preparation of the food items, required for the balanced feeding of dogs with proper vitamin and mineral supplementations in the food.

The cost will not always matter much because the dog's value is being assessed in terms of companionship and the happiness derived from the dog to the dog owner. Though the cost of the food items is comparatively more, many dog owners don't mind much due to the increased benefits derived from their dogs in terms of protection, guiding, etc.

However, the selection of ingredients for homemade food needs to be based on the quality factor. Even when the quality is more, general persons may seek some cheaper items only. Recommended nutrient contents may be obtained from the national nutrient academies in all nations, providing guidelines.

One can correlate the cost factor with items available in their own country. Generally, commercial food items are expensive, especially those that use modern food preparation technologies like oven-baking, sterilization of cans, air drying or freeze-drying of contents, etc.

Canned items cost more than dry food items. However, the cost of the items depends on what kind of food item to be used for the dogs. Food allergies need to be monitored during the usage of different food items in the case of dogs due to the cheaper cost of the items. Often the quality need not be compromised because of the cost factor.

Most of the dog food items nowadays have mentioned their cost in the label itself. Hence, the dog owner need not have any problem in deciding on the purchase.

CHAPTER 6

DRY VS. CANNED FOOD

These types of food materials are different with different grades of liking by the dogs. Dogs like dry foods only if they are tasty only and however, in comparison, the dogs prefer only the canned food items. The reason for such preference by the dogs is that in the case of canned food items, the moisture is about seventy to eighty percent, but only about ten percent in dry food.

However, if you view it in terms of nutrients, often the dry food contains nearly ninety percent nutrients whereas the canned food items include only less percent of nutrients and most of the time. It is only soy products that are structured so well to look like meat pieces.

Hence, to make up the nutritional balance in the body systems, the dog must eat more canned food than dry food. Therefore, compare the cost factor related to this feature by you. Many dry food items are soybean and rice-based.

Now some dry food items are based on corn. Sometimes, beef-based or chicken-based food items come in the cans along with mineral and vitamin supplements suited for the upkeep of the dog's health status. Larger dogs that weigh more than thirty pounds need to be fed with semi-moist food items or dry food items on most occasions.

This is to satisfy the food receptors in the stomach. This is because the larger dogs need to eat plenty of moist food or the canned food items to meet these criteria. But it may not be practically possible in these larger dogs. The small-sized dogs may have a satisfactory level of nutrients if fed even moist food items. However, the caloric density of dry food should not be forgotten. Enriched dry food items are highly welcome than the non - enriched food items.

CHAPTER 7

HOMEMADE DIETS

Homemade diets are essential in dog feeding. Commercial diets often consist of food items with artificial coloring agents and flavoring agents harmful to the dog's body. Homemade food items have the guarantee of freshness in the preparation, unlike ready-made commercial items.

The preservatives added in the commercial food items may not be suitable for the dogs from a health point of view. Even in the case of renal diseases in dogs, the home made diets may be made with ground beef, slices of bread, calcium carbonate, boiled eggs, etc.

The purpose is to have the restricted protein supply in the feed items prepared. This should be carried out with homemade diets formulated exclusively for dogs suffering from renal diseases. Water is added in sufficient quantities to help the proper metabolism in the digestion-impaired renal cases.

The dog may have allergic symptoms like severe itching, which may not get corrected by different medications employed over time. Such cases may get easily treated once the dog food is changed from the commercial type of food to homemade food items.

The homemade food items are often prepared using the freezing procedures to kill the germs or add grape seed extracts to provide sufficient antioxidants to the homemade food items. Food grade vinegar is also added many times to the meat pieces prepared freshly. All these can be enriched with vitamin supplements available in fruit essences, fish oil, etc.

Cranberry juice, bananas, fish, and meat are prepared in a quality manner, and no preservatives are added during the preparation of these kinds of food items. The dog becomes more active after the consumption of such food items.

CHAPTER 8

FOOD ALLERGIES

Food allergies are difficult to identify unless one is well aware of the baseline information about this type of allergy. The main symptoms of food allergies in dogs include facial itching, limb chewing, belly itching, recurrent ear infections, or skin infections.

Since the dogs consume a lot of prepared food materials, including various kinds of proteins, fillers, coloring agents, and more, the incidences of food allergies are more than one can imagine in the commercial food materials. Allergic reactions mainly involve the skin or the gastrointestinal tract.

If you come across your dog itching after providing specific food materials, then suspect the food allergy in this animal. However, conditions like fungal infections need to be ruled out in general before the conclusion of itching as a sign of food allergy.

There are many recorded incidences of allergies of dogs to corn or wheat. However, food allergies vary from dog to dog. Read the labels clearly before feeding your dogs with pet food materials on such occasions. Too many colored food materials may be avoided since they may cause allergies to your dog.

Food allergies are often linked to the hyperactive behavior noticed in dogs. Added colors, preservatives, and a high-fat diet might cause such food allergies in the dogs, and hence, one has to be careful in providing a new kind of diet to their dogs and closely monitor the dog for any signs of allergy.

There are many occasions that food allergies might be diagnosed in the dogs, but the dog may have other problems like pancreatitis. To rule out the food allergies, observe your dogs every time you feed them, look for reasons to link the signs of dog with food given, specific signs encountered, differential diagnosis, etc., are the essential features to be given emphasis.

CHAPTER 9

HOW MUCH SHOULD I FEED
MY DOG?

Many people will give different types of answers based on their experience with their dogs. However, the scientific facts related to the feeding aspects in the case of dogs need to be emphasized the feeding activities maintained in case of dogs.

Usually, the puppies should not be separated before they are eight weeks old. However, sometimes the orphaned puppies may exist. Usually, about five percent of the body weight may be considered criteria for the quantity of food given to the puppies. However, the amount that the dog consumes varies with the size of the dogs also.

However, one can have a thumb rule of feeding the puppy until you see visible fullness of the abdomen to a moderate degree. Suppose you are going on providing the animal without emphasizing the animal's stomach appearance. In that case, the puppy may experience some kinds of digestive upsets, and diarrhea may occur in them.

This may cause many inconveniences to the owner as well as the puppy. Unlike adult dogs, the puppies need to be fed with limited amounts of food but more frequencies. However, once the age advances, the payment may be increased to some extent, but the frequency of feeding is often decreased on many occasions.

A dog on a raw diet may consume only two to four percent of its body weight. Just observe the feeding pattern of the dog and the body condition of the animal closely. If the dog becomes obese, reduce the quantity of food, and if the dog becomes thin, then have an increase in the feeding items.

As mentioned earlier, puppies and adolescent dogs eat more than adult dogs. Likewise, the senior dog eats more petite than the adult dog due to the reduced movements of the dog. However, remember to restrict the amounts of protein during the feeding of the diet to the aged dogs.

41

CHAPTER 10

HOW OFTEN SHOULD I FEED MY DOG?

This often becomes an important question asked by many dog lovers and dog owners. If it is a puppy within the age of the first six weeks, the puppies need to be given milk at the rate of five to seven times per day. The puppy will make some sound if it wants to feed in general.

However, the feeding frequency may be reduced when the dog becomes six to eight weeks old. By the time the dog assumes the age of four weeks, it may start taking some solid food. Hence, mix the solid food with water in the majority and feed your puppy once or twice in the beginning and if the dog develops some diarrhea, then delay the feeding.

It is often due to trial and error but taking some basic steps in feeding, so you need to watch out. The feeding frequency may be changed two to three times after the assumption of the age of eight weeks. However, if the dog is seen hungry, craving for food, then provide food once than the estimated numbers. This varies with different breeds of dogs.

However, avoid feeding too many times in this age group of dogs. Around three months to six months of age, the puppy will be teething. Hence, restrict the feeding to two times only, but the balanced type of nutrition needs to be provided to the dogs of this age group to avoid the deficiency-based symptoms in them.

From six months to one year, try using puppy food that is available commercially. However, from first-year onwards, the adult food may be given gradually. However, when the dog becomes an elder dog, restrict the frequency of feeding since the movements of such adult dogs are highly reduced due to multiple reasons. However, the pregnant animal may be fed extra time depending on the animal's willingness and restrict the quantity of the food without compromising food quality.

CHAPTER 11

SIGNS OF ILL HEALTH

Signs of ill health are the most important signs of the health status of your dogs. For example, if the dog has continuous nasal discharge, it indicates nasal congestion, and if the shot is thick, most of the time, the dog may have pneumonia.

If the dog vomits one or two times occasionally, this may not be taken as a serious sign of ill health, but if the dog continues this vomiting, then this is something significant to be looked into.

If the dog has continuous itching, then one needs to check up the dog first by closer observation and skin examination by separating the hair material, especially in long-haired breeds. You may also come across many ticks or lice on the skin, which may look standard at a distance.

If the dog passes loose stool one or two times, this need not be given more emphasis, but if there is continuous passing of loose stool, then the dog is understood to suffer from bowel disorders. If the dog does not pass stool for two to three days, the digestive upsets need to be ruled out carefully.

Just patiently observe the dog's walking movements and rule out any abnormal movements in the dog. If the dog is limping, the animal may have foot lesions. Similarly, if the aged dog has reluctant walking and less feed intake along with repeated vomiting, then acute renal disorders like nephritis need to be ruled out.

If there is whiteness in the eyes, suspect the corneal opacity that may occur in diseases like trypanosomosis. When the dog becomes anemic, the mucous membrane of the eyes becomes paler, and in severe cases, this may have a white wall color. If the dog bites chain and owners or others, look for behavior disorders, and rabies needs to be ruled out.

CHAPTER 12

HEARTWORM, FLEAS,
AND OTHER PARASITES

Heartworm, fleas, and other parasites in dogs need to be eliminated by following appropriate medications in them. Many products have come up in the commercial fields to protect the dogs from heartworms, fleas, and other parasites like hookworms, whipworms, roundworms, lice, ticks, etc.

Among the heartworm, fleas, and other parasites, the fleas produce hypersensitive reactions in the affected animals. Hence, the animals infected with fleas start severely scratching bodies. The scratching is so severe that the skin becomes more hyperemic, and dermatitis occurs in the affected areas.

The animal will not lie down or sleep comfortably due to the constant bites by the fleas. Hence, the animal looks as if affected by some severe skin disease. Suppose the animal is not adequately attended to this tick bite problem. In that case, there will often be secondary bacterial invasions in these sites, and there may even be a foul smell emanating from the skin areas.

Close observation of the dog is highly essential to rule out fleas disturbing the animal to a greater extent. Similarly, the animal's skin needs to be tested for ticks, lice, etc. For this, the hair materials need to be separated, and close observation with patience is required for the proper diagnosis.

In many incidences, if anemia is present, the blood protozoa need to be ruled out in addition to the hookworm problems. The dog owners themselves might recognize the clinical issues like anemia, loose motion, pot belly, etc... However, the dog needs to undergo routine health-related examinations involving fecal examination, hematological examination, and blood smear examination.

Many commercial products have come up in the market, which is helpful to deal with all these conditions by a single dose. Drugs like ivermectin are beneficial and are available in both injection and oral form and the solution form applied on the skin. These drugs in dogs can lead to the prevention of these conditions also.

53

CHAPTER 13

HEARTWORM PREVENTION

Beef flavored chunks are available in addition to the beef flavored tablets or solutions that can be given orally to the dogs as a measure against the incidence of heartworms. Avoid mosquito bites by providing proper mosquito-proof shelter facilities to the dogs.

Just plan whether there is any need to go for heartworm prevention throughout the year or only in some months. For example, in some countries, the mosquitoes may be dormant in most of the colder months.

However, in some countries, this is not a position. Many times, medications are available for oral administration to prevent heartworms along with hookworms, etc. Such oral medications need to be taken as per the instructions. However, be cautious about any adverse drug reactions in the dog given with such prophylactic therapy.

Adverse event reports need to be sent if you come across any sorts of adverse drug reactions in your dog during the preventive treatment.

The pet animals highly prefer soft beef-flavored tablets as the preventive measure against heartworms. The pet owner needs to consult a veterinarian if the dose for heartworm prevention is missed for few months. On such occasions, the pet animal needs to undergo a heartworm test.

Heartgard, sentinel, interceptor, revolution, etc., are available in the commercial fields as drugs for preventive measure. Avoid water stagnation around the dog shelter and the bushes around the area that facilitate mosquito breeding. This test needs to be carried out in consultation with a veterinarian specializing in pet animal health care and medicine.

As a preventive measure for heartworms, the dogs need to be tested for evidence of these worms at the age of six months. Natural beef chewable tablets are available containing medical agents like ivermectin.

CHAPTER 14

COMMON QUESTIONS
ABOUT HEARTWORM

The common questions about heartworm are often related to the species affected by heartworms in addition to the dogs. One should know that dogs, the cat, fox, wolf, horse, sea lion, etc. are also affected. Can this be cured or not? Yes. This can be treated.

What is the drug used often for the prevention of heartworm in dogs? Ivermectin is the drug used often to have preventive actions for these heartworms. Dogs affected reveal constant coughing, panting, and dullness on many occasions.

What will be the size of the worms? In the case of the females, it is about twenty-seven centimeters, and in the case of males, it is about seventeen centimeters in length. Is there any vector involved in the transmission of the disease? Yes. Mosquitoes often get associated as

vectors in which the early development of larvae of heartworms occur in them.

Is the prophylaxis meant only for heartworms or others also?   The prevention is intended not only for the heartworms but also for the hookworms, whipworms, and roundworms. What is the infective type of larvae that is associated with the transmission of these heartworms? Mosquito bites transmit the third stage larva.

This occurs throughout the world. In some areas, the incidences are less in colder months in which the mosquito breeding will not be there and maybe dormant during these periods. What is the name of the drug used for therapy and prevention? Ivermectin and milbemycin oxime may be used for both purposes. Ivermectin is available in injection form and oral forms.

Additionally, the forms for external applications are also available. The cost factor needs to be worked out for all these treatments. What is the frequency of drugs used for prevention? One month before the mosquito season and up to two months after the mosquito season, ivermectin or milbemycin oxime may be given once monthly for prevention. Diethylcarbamazine may be used for therapy purposes.

CHAPTER 15

FLEAS AND OTHER PARASITES

Fleas and other parasites need to be constantly given priority by the dog owners. The common incidences of flea bite allergy in the case of dogs cause worries among dog owners. Flea bite induces allergic reactions in the concerned area bitten by the fleas. Hence, the affected area looks like a hairless area, and the animal starts scratching.

Fleas cause severe dermatitis in dogs with severe flea infestations. Many times, the flea bite causes allergic reactions in the dogs. On many occasions, dogs experience severe discomforts due to these allergic reactions. Medicated collars are available to treat and prevent the infestation with external parasites like ticks or fleas.

Other parasites like ticks, lice, and internal parasites like hookworms, roundworms, whipworms, etc., cause affections in the animal's health status. For example, if hookworm affects the animal, most of the time, the dog has anemia. The anemic signs become more prominent depending on the degree of affection by the hookworm.

Hookworm larvae can pass directly through the skin and cause problems in the affected ones. Such dogs may reveal lesions about dermatitis in the feet region and the skin areas. Skin rashes may be seen frequently in such cases, and the affected animal passes loose stool, which is red-tinged and mixed with blood material.

If the roundworms are seen in more numbers, the affected puppies reveal a potbelly condition easily recognized by the dog owners themselves. Piperazine salts are given by oral route for the treatment of this problem. However, broad-spectrum anthelmintics like pyrantel pamoate, fenbendazole, etc., are presented to treat these conditions.

Many drugs have come in the market to treat fleas and other parasites. Nowadays, the medical agent called many dog owners highly prefer ivermectin to treat fleas and other parasites in dogs. This drug is available in injection form and oral forms. Even the drug is available for external application also.

CHAPTER 16

DO PARASITES CAUSE "SCOOTING"?

Parasites to cause the scooting. Scooting is an anal sac disease. First, let's understand what rushing is in detail. This is the dragging of the anus with the hind limbs in an extended state. Parasites irritating the anus regions lead to such types of actions in animals like dogs.

However, one should not be under the impression that it is the parasite that alone causes such scooting in the case of dogs. There are many occasions in which the dog may have the scooting without any parasite-based etiological agent. For example, anal gland infections, tumors at the anus, and injuries near the anal regions also may lead to such type of dragging of anus region, frequently by the affected dogs.

Flea bite allergy often irritates the anus region. The animal may try to bite the anus region, and the irritations due to these factors lead to the final dragging of the anus region on the ground. Cestodiasis in dogs is a condition caused by tapeworms.

On such occasions, if the animal is not treated in time, the animal may exhibit scooting activities. Tapeworm segments passed in the stool create crawling-like activities near the anus.

Such crawling activities of the tapeworm segments lead to severe itching at these regions. Hence, to relieve this constant irritation, the animal starts pressing the anus region on the ground first and then tries to drag it on the floor with a typical rear limb extension.

Usually, there is a packet of eggs when the fecal sample is examined by microscope. However, the flotation technique leads to the breakage of these packets to burst, and hence, diagnosis is difficult on such occasions. Scooting dogs need to be examined to rule out tapeworm segments, which look like rice-like pieces.

These segments are white and turn yellow when taken from the body. Tapeworms themselves may be seen in the motion or near the anus below the tail regions. Consult your veterinarian for specific cures for this.

CHAPTER 17

PREVENTING DENTAL DISEASE

Preventing dental disease is an important feature, which is to be paid more emphasis by dog lovers or dog owners. Dental disease is given priority in the dog's health schedule nowadays because of the association of dental diseases with systemic diseases.

Antibiotics need to be given in the initial stage of teeth infection itself. If not, this may cause specific conditions, and the organisms may spread to the other nearby regions like the oral mucous membrane and pharyngeal region, etc.

More acidic or alkaline food materials need not be given to the dogs to avoid possible teeth damage. Antibiotics need to be shown in the initial stage of teeth infection itself. If not, this may cause specific conditions, and the organisms may spread to the other nearby regions like the oral mucous membrane and pharyngeal region, etc. More acidic or alkaline food materials need not be given to the dogs to avoid possible teeth damage. If the dog is not presented at its young age with some bony material to bite on, it may develop some dental diseases later. The teething action often causes the animal to go for grinding indiscriminately. Hence, the animal has to be given some biting materials to avoid the occurrence of dental diseases.

If there is evidence of bleeding from the oral region, the dog must be examined thoroughly for any dental abnormality. Mainly the puppies or sometimes the adult dogs also may have teeth injuries. They need to be attended to immediately as a preventive step.

If not, the animal may end up in secondary bacterial infections.

Hunting dogs need additional care associated with the dental structures, and such consideration is required to avoid future dental problems in such dogs. Brushes are available to provide better dental care to dogs. However, one has to allot more time and have the patience to use such brushes in dogs. This may lead to further problems. Centers for disease control and prevention are trying to put up guidelines to prevent dental diseases in dogs in many nations. However, the oral examination needs to be carried out frequently in dogs, and such activities help to rule out the emerging problems about the dentine structures at the beginning itself.

CHAPTER 18

HOME DENTAL CARE

Home dental care is to be given more emphasis nowadays because dental diseases are emerging in pet animals like dogs to a greater extent. Though you are providing home dental care, if you suspect the extension of the dental diseases, immediately approach the veterinarian for intervention.

Try to provide bone materials without very sharp points to the dogs, and they may love to chew them and then swallow the bitten products. Such activities help them to go for the development of solid teeth structures naturally.

Mind that the breeds of dogs like Pekingese, etc., are more prone to developing teeth diseases because the teeth are closely crowned in the oral cavity be to the small size of these dogs. Hence, these dogs need to be checked up for excessive plaque formation in the home itself.

Recreational raw beef bones are beautiful materials to keep the teeth structures of your dog clean and free from the formation of plaque with the build-up of bacterial organisms. Teeth brushes are available for use with care in the case of dogs, and one has to be careful during the usage of these brushes in dogs. Teeth brushes are to be used with particular kinds of pastes recommended by the veterinarians for home use in dogs.

Specially prepared food materials are available in the pet shops to remove the tartar and the plaque materials from the teeth structures.

Dry dog food and toys specially made to add strength to the teeth structures are often used at home for better teeth cleaning.

The plaque materials are intermittent to be removed at home to avoid any periodontal diseases, which are more common among dogs. Dental wipes are available in pet shops, and they may be used carefully in the home. This helps to remove more plaque and the tartar-like materials that are loosely attached.

CHAPTER 19

VETERINARY DENTAL TREATMENTS

Veterinary dental treatments are more important. If the dental structures are not being looked at carefully, there are more chances to develop periodontal diseases in dogs. Hence, veterinary dental treatments need to be paid maximum importance during the life of your dogs.

Many advanced systems deal with dental treatments that have come up in the market. Many methods are available with built-in water spray systems, double filter systems, autoclavable clips, and more.

Many veterinarians use high-speed fiber-optic handpieces with push-button turbines, two-hand piece water jet systems, soundless water compressors, and more. The diagnosis of a condition about the periodontal structure-based diseases is more important before the treatment.

Periodontal diseases are graded into minimal and moderate, and severe conditions. Accordingly, the therapy is carried out, and it is impossible to check all teeth by essential oral examination in the dog patient. Hence, general anesthesia is required before the assessment of the teeth inside structures. Surgical curettage is done in case of advanced periodontal diseases using flaps. The teeth extractions are also carried out using moderate force, and more care is taken to avoid continuous bleeding.

Oral surgeries are undertaken after obtaining the dogs' dental radiographs and comparing tissue damage with typical teeth structures. The concerned veterinarians assess the extent of damage in a systematic manner.

Periodontal diseases are controlled by the administration of broad-spectrum antibiotics effectively. Along with dental surgeries, oral treatment is done with many products that are helpful to prevent the attachment of tartar or plaque on the teeth. However, reputable products should be used in the veterinary practice, and the dog owner's satisfaction is given more priority during veterinary dental therapy.

CHAPTER 20

THE IMPORTANCE OF THE PHYSICAL EXAMINATION

The importance of the physical examination need not be underestimated in the case of dogs. Simple but systematic physical examination techniques may diagnose most of the disorders in dogs. Hence, without physical examination of the dog, one should not resort to knowing the status of your dog's health.

Observe the dog with scratching. Catch the dog and separate the hair material from the itching site. To the surprise, you may come across a big wound on the ground site. The damage might be the main reason for the scratching of the dog at that site. However, one has to rule out the occurrence of the wound by severe itching itself.

Many times, when the scratching dog is examined physically, one can come across plenty of lice infestation or tick problems in the skin and coat. The parasitic condition might not be diagnosed at all if one has not carried out the physical examination. Similarly, the dog may reveal the signs of pain when the physical analysis is carried out by deep palpation technique. The dog show signs of pain when the dog is examined at the stomach or the back regions.

Even if it is possible that by pressure-based palpation, one can detect the acute renal disorders in the affected dogs turn to the examined site at the kidney or the back region. The dog affected by Cystitis with severe retention of urine is often diagnosed by mere physical examination.

The filled bladder, together with signs of pain during the examination at the site of the urinary bladder, indicates that the animal is affected by Cystitis. Auscultation of the heart on both right and left sides helps to rule out abnormal heart sounds. The pulmonary area-based auscultation reveals respiratory system disorders like pneumonia.

CHAPTER 21

WHY ARE REGULAR CHECKUPS IMPORTANT?

Why are regular checkups important? Every dog owner asks this type of question often. If you failed to do the regular checkups, the dog might have some significant diseases you don't know about. Hence, you need to pay a lot of money to the veterinarians for consultancy and the required drugs useful for the therapy of the clinical condition.

One may not find out the very commonly occurring clinical conditions in their dogs because of less experience with dog diseases or dog rearing. This is why checkups are essential. For example, if the dog has a potbelly, the condition may not look abnormal many times. But if the dog is subjected to a regular checkup, the veterinarian immediately finds it out and gives the appropriate therapy. If not, the animal may experience diarrhea and dehydration.

If the dog has any signs of illness, then don't wait for the regular checkup. Instead, you need to approach the veterinarian immediately. If done regularly, checkups will help vaccinations against canine distemper, parvovirus, coronavirus, rabies virus, hepatitis virus, and more.

Booster vaccinations will be carried out in such cases without any delay in the injections. This helps to improve the immunity level of the dog against such diseases to a remarkable degree. Regular checkup is the essential one with proper stools examination. Hence, the deworming may be carried out with drugs like fenbendazole, albendazole, etc.

Abnormalities like signs of pain may be ruled out during such examinations. If not, helminthiasis may affect the animal, and diarrhea may occur in addition to the other types of digestive upsets and anemia. Regular inspections help to rule out external parasitic conditions like lice or tick infestations. Dental problems are also found out during regular checkups in reputed veterinary hospitals.

CHAPTER 22

WHAT HAPPENS DURING AN EXAMINATION?

This question often looks so simple but holds more meanings in that. During your dog's examination, you need to prepare the dog first psychologically for a better-restrained status. For this, you need to take a leash and place the dog on the table by the careful delivery of unified command.

When the dog is trying to avoid a thorough examination by the veterinarian, try to distract the dog by simply scratching your dog behind the ears. Hence, the dog's attention is somewhat diverted from the examination procedures carried out often in a systematic manner.

However, there are obedient dogs, which will remain calm during an examination. Such dogs need to be given some patting on the shoulder or the body and praises. Perhaps, many owners may try to provide some treats that are liked so much by the concerned dogs. However, it all depends on the training offered to the concerned dog earlier and the effective follow-up procedures by the owner for the maintenance of such reflexes during the examination.

Muzzles are required for some dogs if they behave differently by objecting to the examination procedures by the frequent movements of the body or trying to bite the veterinarian examining the dog. Hence, the owner needs to observe the dog closely during the examination to rule out any abnormal activity by the dog.

Restraining activities properly during the clinical examination of the dog is highly appreciable if they are successful with the concerned dogs. Such control will be beneficial for examining the patient by the concerned veterinarian in the pet clinic.

If the dog gets more distracted during examination using restlessness, one may even use the electronic equipment, making some sound that is audible to the dogs' ear. Such things will be helpful in the proper distraction of the animal during the examination.

CHAPTER 23

HOW OFTEN SHOULD
MY PET BE EXAMINED?

Most dog owners try to find this answer seriously. Whatever the schedule we have for examining your pet animal, if there is any abnormality noticed in your animal, you need to subject the animal for a thorough clinical examination without delay. Even before purchasing a puppy, it can be suggested to consult a pet animal care specialist and try to understand the schedules to be maintained to examine the animal. This will help a lot in solving many health-related problems in the concerned animal.

Though once in two or three months is the general schedule for examining the dog, the dog needs to be taken to the veterinarian for a thorough examination as soon as the puppy is procured. Hence, the health care measures related program will be obtained in time. Most of the time, the dog is to be taken to the veterinarian at the fifth or sixth week of age. In this period only, the vaccinations against diseases will be systematically carried out. The vaccination period in the first year will be continued up to the sixteenth week of age, and the schedule needs to be maintained accordingly.

However, if you have a pregnant dog, the dog need not be stressed by long-distance-based transportation for examination purposes. Hence, consult the veterinarian by phone and try to reduce the travel for the dog. However, veterinary advice needs to be obtained in terms of health maintenance. If the dog has met with an accident either during travel or during routine movements, the animal must immediately be taken to the pet hospital.

Though no disease is evident, it does not mean that the dog is healthy. There are occasions wherein the animal may look like an average dog but may have some diseases, which can be found during routine health checkups. Hence, the owner has to decide when to take the dog to the hospital depending on necessity.

CHAPTER 24

HOW TO ADMINISTER MEDICINE

Most of the time, the dogs are so intelligent to find out the dog owners' drug mixed water or food materials. Hence, often it becomes a headache for the dog owners to give medicines to their dogs. To the possible extent, the animal need not be forced to take the drug. If the treatment is to be provided by mouth, decide whether it is better to give it water or food. The medicines are often mixed with food materials and are kept in concealed positions by adequately mixing the mixture with the food materials.

Before administering the medicine, delay the feeding time in the particular dog. Hence, the dog may be hungry to some extent. At that time, give little quantity of regular food without medicine, and the dog may eat it well without any suspicion and now provide the treatment mixed food. The dog may voluntarily eat it most of the time if the dog resists, first restraining the dog well and opening the mouth. Place the tablet behind the fang teeth and almost behind the bulb of the tongue. However, take care that you are administering in the dog should not enter directly into the respiratory organ like the lungs.

If so, the dog will experience many bouts-like activities and may end up in aspiration pneumonia with severe nasal discharge and panting-like activities. In puppies, swab the medicine around the upper lip. The puppy will lick the drug automatically by the tongue. Hence, the administration becomes perfect in such cases.

If the medicine is in liquid form, don't raise the dog's head too much and place the medication by a syringe. Just by using a dropper, fill the medicine in the slip pocket. The continuous rubbing at the throat side may stimulate the swallowing. Making the animal thirsty and then offering treatment mixed water may often help the intake of the medicine.

CHAPTER 25

NURSING A SICK DOG

Nursing a sick dog is one of the vital measures that a dog owner needs to understand. Similarly, when a dog becomes ill, the dog needs more care and affection-based activities by the dog owners. Nursing a sick animal is often considered an art, which should not be regarded as a causal measure.

Yes. You need to take extra care of the dog when it becomes sick. For example, the sick dog with a high fever needs to be given only some bread pieces, and bulky non-vegetarian items may be avoided. Such dogs should be kept in some calm place after medications are taken and should not be disturbed. During the nursing of the dog who has taken the drug, the animal needs coaxing and stroking by the owner. Don't raise the dog's head too much to avoid passing medicines given by the mouth directly into the respiratory organs like the lungs. During the nursing measures, take care by giving warm fluids.

Safety is to be given more priority during the nursing activity in any dog. When the dog has severe diarrhea, the animal may start showing signs of dehydration. Hence, the nursing care for dehydration includes small doses of salt and glucose to water carefully.

Similarly, the vomiting dog also needs proper nursing care. Ice cubes may be given in such cases along with egg whites to smooth the esophageal passage.

Nowadays, a non-contact-based infrared thermometer has come up in the market to obtain the animal's temperature without much stress. Place the dog in a shaded place if the weather is high and provide good ventilation to the suffering animal. If the animal is suffering from hypothermia, provide warm blankets to given comfort to the animal.

CHAPTER 26

VACCINATIONS

Vaccinations need to be always undertaken by the pet owners, and the dogs need to be vaccinated at the appropriate time. This helps to improve the resistance of the animal against some specific diseases causing frequent problems in dogs. The dogs that are orphaned due to the mother's death have lesser protection in their immune system.

Such animals are to be particularly protected against various diseases.

Vaccination is usually started at the age of five to six weeks, and before this age, the maternal immunity will be helping the animal to have natural disease resistance. It is always better to deworm the animal before the vaccination, and this is given emphasis many times. Vaccination against the parvovirus is done early because pups are often being affected by parvoviral infections. The booster dose for each vaccine needs to be given at the appropriate time, which helps build up the immune status in an appreciable manner. Vaccination is carried out in many countries against rabies disease.

Hence, vaccination against rabies is given more emphasis always. Even rabies tags are fixed onto the dog collar of most of the dogs. The rabies vaccine is provided at the age of thirteen to fifteenth weeks of age and repeated in the fifteenth months. However, this depends on the type of vaccine used. Once in three years, this is repeated.

In dogs that have not received colostrums or dogs at high-risk areas, give a measles virus vaccine and kill parvovirus vaccines before five weeks of age. Leptospira serovar vaccine is given at six to eight weeks of age and again at tenth to twelfth weeks and thirteenth to sixteenth weeks.

Then annually repeat this. Bordetella and Lyme disease vaccinations are only optional ones in the case of dogs. Vaccinations against the canine parainfluenza, canine parvovirus, and canine adenovirus type-two are similar to the schedule maintained with leptospiral serovars.

CHAPTER 27

COMMON QUESTIONS
ABOUT VACCINATIONS

Common questions about vaccinations are to be understood by the dog owners as a priority. One of the common questions is whether the dog needs to be given vaccination on the first week of age or not. The dogs need not be vaccinated within five to six weeks of age. But, if they did not receive vaccinations, then the vaccination against the parvoviral infections used to kill viral vaccines and measles disease may be given.

Another common question is whether the dog is given a bordetella disease vaccine and Lyme disease vaccine. No, these vaccines are only optional. Can the parvoviral vaccine be used in the first week of life? No. This will interfere with maternal antibody levels.

Can a pregnant animal be vaccinated? Yes. Two to three weeks earlier to pregnancy activity that is expected, the pregnant animal may be vaccinated against viral diseases. This helps to provide maternal antibodies to the young one to be given birth. Is there any need to give rabies vaccine to dogs? Yes. It is a must to go for the anti-rabies vaccine for dogs.

When this anti-rabies vaccine is given to the dogs, what precaution does one need to undertake in this regard? The rabies vaccine is provided at the age of thirteen to fifteen weeks of age and should be repeated in fifteen months and then once in three years. The dog must be given this vaccine.

However, this depends on the risk area. Is there any need for canine distemper vaccination in the case of dogs? Yes. There is a specific requirement in the case of dogs for the immunization against the canine distemper. This disease is more prevalent in most countries.

Is there any vaccination against leptospirosis, and at what age the dog is to be vaccinated? This is to be given at the period of six to eight weeks of age, again at tenth to twelfth weeks, and again at thirteenth to sixteenth weeks of age.

CHAPTER 28

SPAYING AND NEUTERING

Spaying and neutering of dogs are highly wanted if you don't want to breed the dogs. However, these activities need to be carried out by qualified veterinarians specialized in pet care and management. Anesthesia is required along with due surgical procedures for carrying out the spaying and neutering.

One has to understand first the terms like spaying or neutering. Both are related to the surgical approaches of sterilization in the case of females and males, respectively. However, the term neutering is also associated with such procedures in both sexes. These procedures can highly minimize accidental pregnancies that are not wanted.

Spaying and neutering help prevent pyometra occurrence, which is a common reproductive disorder-giving problem to dog owners. In male dogs, neutering helps to prevent the occurrence of prostate enlargement or cancer. Hence, these help to minimize the incidences of reproductive disorders in dogs.

By these spaying and neutering, the male dog's desire in search of a female dog in heat is highly minimized, and hence, the wandering of a male dog is reduced. The animal becomes calm also by these surgical remedies. Territorial behavior of these animals is also highly minimized by these in the case of male dogs.

Spaying your dog before the occurrence of the first heat is the best one to avoid the incidence of breast cancer. If the dog is fixed after the first heat, the chances of breast cancer in them are more and has been proved by research. The younger group of dogs need to be subjected to these operations to avoid complications in the future.

Many veterinarians prefer the spaying and neutering of dogs only at the age of five to six years. However, these can be performed even at the age of three to five years. Postoperative care needs to be followed meticulously to avoid the occurrence of infections by microbial organisms.

CHAPTER 29

SPAYING OF THE FEMALE DOG

Spaying of the female dog is undertaken to control unwanted pregnancy by crossing some unknown or country or non-descript dogs. The spaying of the dog reduces the aggressiveness of the dog. By spaying, one can reduce the incidences of commonly encountered reproductive diseases like pyometra.

Spaying also helps control stray animals, and many nations are doing these operations by removing the ovaries from the female animals. Experienced veterinarians are required to do the spaying in female dogs, and postoperative care to be given more emphasis. Suppose proper control measures are not taken after the surgical operation for the removal of an ovary. In that case, the infections may start setting in, and the animal may end up in the development of peritonitis, and then toxemia sets in, causing unwanted health problems.

The dog's death may finally occur if the dog is not provided effective and proper veterinary care. A female dog spayed before the occurrence of first heat will have almost zero chance of developing mammary cancer, which is more familiar with the dogs that are not fixed.

A female dog generally comes to heat once in eight months or so. During the heat, bleeding from the vagina and the dog may cross with the unwanted male, and the spaying activity prevents all these. In the case of aged dogs, the dog may often get signs of increased thirst, anorexia, vomiting, etc., that are so common with pyometra.

Pyometra means the presence of pus in the uterus. Once pyometra occurs, it involves many discomforts to the animal and the cost factor involved for the therapy. Such pyometra is prevented by spaying because, in spaying, you are removing both ovaries and the uterus.

CHAPTER 30

SURGICAL NEUTERING
OF THE MALE DOG

Surgical neutering of the male dog is essential in helping the dog owners to control the male dog's aggressive behavior. Yes. It becomes possible to control the dog's restlessness by doing the surgical neutering, which might have caused so much agony for the owner. Hence, neutering corrects such activity to the benefit of the dog owner.

When the dog is in the puppy stage, the dog may be subjected to the surgical neutering technique. Hence, the hormonal impact is highly minimized in such male dogs.

The surgical neutering of the male dog helps to prevent the incidences of prostate gland diseases. Generally, in the case of male dogs, prostate enlargement is more common. In canine patients who have undergone surgical neutering, the incidences of such prostate enlargement are minimized.

Sometimes, the adult male dog has more difficulties during defecation. However, one has to rule out feed-borne constipation like lack of fibers, etc., before resorting to the fixation of prostate enlargement as a cause for this. Constipation is mainly due to the increased size of the prostate gland. Neutering makes shrinkage of the prostate gland. In surgical neutering, the incision is placed in front of the scrotum, and the testicles are removed in a surgical manner using aseptic techniques.

The wound need not be closed except the tying up of the cord after cutting the testicle. However, in two to three days, some swelling may occur in the scrotum as a normal tissue reaction. However, once you administer the antibiotic with a broader spectrum of activities, the condition gets recovered in a satisfactory condition. Septic shock may occur if the surgical site gets infected with some microbial infections. In these cases, the wound needs a thorough dressing procedure, and the patient needs to be continuously monitored in a clinical environment.

Please take note that local animal organizations perform surgical neutering when they capture stray male dogs.

CHAPTER 31

PET HEALTH INSURANCE

Pet health insurance is highly required nowadays because of the escalating cost factors about the health maintenance in dogs and other animals. Dog owners need to find pet insurance firms that settle dues to the pet owners without much delay and in a more appropriate manner. Pet health insurance firms recently come forward to pay the rights correctly after the due verification of the claim. If anything happens, dog care costs can add up without insurance.

Hence, know the approved list of your local animal care hospitals. Even have a list of veterinary experts specializing in dog health care and disease management measures. Many firms cover up the cost of undertaking surgeries, radiographic examinations, treatment of specific conditions, laboratory fees towards undertaking various laboratory examinations, and more. Before accepting your policy by most insurance firms after enrolling from you, there is a weighting period before taking your approach, so it's good to start early.

If you don't like the insurance firm, at any time, you can cancel the insurance policy. A licensed veterinarian list should be available with all insurance firms. Many payment options are available for pet owners.

It is better to enroll the dogs or other pets before they become adults. The animals, when they are young, need to be registered as a priority.
It is always better for the consumers who are dog owners. Before the dogs have any illness,

accidents, or get into pre-existing conditions, as quoted by many pet health insurance firms, insurance coverage needs to be entered by the dog owners. Your dog's medical history will be subjected to full review by the insurance firms, so start soon.

CHAPTER 32

CLIPPING A DOG

Many dog owners generally think of clipping as only a mechanical activity. Few understand that clipping a dog is an art. Cutting a coat or nail needs to be carried out carefully to avoid injuries to the skin or nail. Clipping of the coat is to be taken care of as per the breed characteristics. If the coat is not clipped correctly, this may lead to dust accumulation in the coat, and the animal may start showing signs of skin diseases. This is true, especially when the grooming activities are not done correctly.

Clipping of coat helps to get rid of the parasitic burden to a greater extent, and also, the clipping of your dog is more beneficial to expose the type of parasitic problem that the dog is likely to suffer. Many pet health parlors are available, wherein the clipping of dogs will be carried out more systematically.

Always make use of a sharp clipper, and in the winter regions, avoid the close clipping. This is because the more immediate clipping in the winter seasons may expose the dog to environmental stresses like the cold climate. Hence, the dog may become more vulnerable to frostbite. Avoid the close clipping of coat or nail because this may cause injury to the underlying tissues and may cause bleeding in the concerned animal.

Many pet owners need to avoid any clipping activity when the animal is not in nutritional status. Clipping instruments are available to a greater extent in many pet shops. Avoid the blunt instruments because they may not clip well, and hence, repetition is required often.

Always use modern equipment for clipping activities.

CHAPTER 33

FIRST STEPS IN GROOMING

Grooming is one of the essential activities to be known well by the dog owner. If the dog owner is not aware of the grooming, the dog may encounter many diseases. The first steps of grooming consist of activities like maintenance of coat, nails, and ears. The maintenance of the coat mainly consists of enrichment measures like proper bathing, combing, drying of skin by dryers, and more. The animal needs not to be bathed daily, which helps protect the skin's characteristics like insulation feature.

Use conditioners and shampoos that are meant for dogs. Combing needs to be carried out with a soft brush meant for use in the case of dogs. There are varieties of bushes available, and depending on the type of breeds, one can use the concerned brush. This grooming of the coat by a comb needs to be carried out daily, and the fallen hair, if any, needs to be placed in a dust bin always.

Otherwise, when the dog owners switch on the fan, the hair will fly and enter the nostrils of persons. Always don't clip too much because this may lead to injuries of nails always. Similarly, you need to carry all the materials required for the clipping with you before starting the procedure.

Use a sharp clipper designed for use in the case of dogs. It is better to have the dog in the raised place, and hence, the control of the animal is easier. Ear canals are to be checked up frequently, and sterile cotton may be used for cleaning purposes. Grooming-associated guidelines need to be followed strictly by the dog owners.

Nail maintenance is one of the first steps of grooming activities. Live nail areas can be easily clipped away and are always light-colored than the reddish area of the nail in the higher position. During the holding of your dog's feet by you, always have a firm grip. If not, the dog will take the upper hand during the clipping, and some injury may occur.

CHAPTER 34

BATHING A DOG

Bathing a dog needs to be given more emphasis. This is because if you are careless in bathing, the animal may end up having some infections. For example, if you don't close the ears with a large cotton ball, the water may enter into ear canals and cause ear infections with signs like constant discharge from the ears and shaking of the head.

The frequency of bathing depends on the breed of the dog. If the dog is of a hairy type like the cocker spaniel, then the bathing will be carried out once in six to eight weeks. If these breeds are bathed too frequently, then the skin and coat lose the protective characters. However, when the dog has defecated on the skin due to the frequent digestive upsets leading to diarrhea, to avoid the bad smell, the dog may be subjected to regular bathing sometimes by the owners.

Take more care in avoiding some irritant soaps or human soaps. The soap materials used for human beings are not suitable for dogs. Similarly, many human shampoo products have some ingredients that are not suitable in the proportions that are to be used in the case of dogs. Hence, always try to use the shampoo products that are mentioned mainly for use in dogs. Take more care in using any new product.

Always have good time and patience for products required for bathing in one place with water source availability. Dogs love the sprinkling of water, river, and oceans. Even when you are using the bathtub, have everything in one place and then start bathing the dog. Try to have a leash, conditioner, towel, and shampoo in the bath place.

Conditioner is helpful to make the combing activity easier later. Bathing should be a convenient activity for both the dog and the owner. This should not be a burden.

CHAPTER 35

PET IDENTIFICATION

Pet identification is highly required these days because of the need for the licensing of the dog in a proper manner and to reduce the number of stray dog menace in streets. Pet identification is made by many methods, which are different from each other. The cost factor for that also has variations accordingly.

The identification of your pet may be made by personalized tags, sometimes by the municipal license tag, rabies tag, and more. Most of the time, your telephone number and name will be placed in the personalized tags of the dogs. If anybody encounters the dog accidentally during the event of missing, the dog will become capable of reporting the facts to the concerned officials.

Plastic and metal pet identification tags are available in multiple colors, and the dog owners can choose the color they want. However, many select the reflective type of dog tags along with the collars. Hence, the dogs can be identified even in darkness to a greater extent.

Nowadays, many electronic gadgets are available, like microchips which are embedded into the dog. However, these kinds of electronic chips need to be implanted behind the ears, and once planted, this will reveal all the data embedded in this in the computer. Collard and tagged animal indicate that it is not a stray animal, which gives more security to the dog.

Traditional forms of identification of animal-like tattooing are now a day not carried in dogs. Thus tracing the missed animal will become more accessible for the pet owners due to the identification-based dog collars.

CPSIA information can be obtained
at www.ICGtesting.com
Printed in the USA
BVHW092335240621
610373BV00006B/1611